BOXER BOOKS Ltd. and the distinctive Boxer Books logo
are trademarks of Union Square & Co., LLC.
Union Square & Co., LLC, is a subsidiary of Sterling Publishing Co., Inc.

Text © 2024 Boxer Books
Illustrations © 2024 Pintachan

First published in North America in 2024.

ISBN 978-1-915801-62-3

Library of Congress Control Number: 2023943676

For information about custom editions, special sales, and premium purchases,
please contact specialsales@unionsquareandco.com.

Printed in China
Lot #: 10 9 8 7 6 5 4 3 2 1

11/23

unionsquareandco.com

Spring Street™ Series created by David Bennett
Written by Sasha Morton
Illustrated by Pintachan
Series editors: Sasha Morton and Leilani Sparrow
Series consultant: Mary Anne Wolpert, Bank Street College of Education

JOBS
Contents

Spring Street

Emergency!

1 Coast guards make sure people and boats are safe at sea.

2 Firefighters work fast to put out fires and stop them from spreading.

Emergency services are the people we call when something goes wrong. They help to keep us safe wherever we are. The three main emergency services are police, paramedics, and firefighters, but perhaps you've seen some of these other first responders in action, too?

4 Lifeboat rescue teams save people who get into trouble out at sea.

5 Fire and rescue helicopters put out fires and get people to safety.

3 Paramedics take care of sick or injured people before they get to the hospital.

6 Police officers prevent crime and keep our streets safe.

1 coast guards

2 firefighter

3 paramedic

4 lifeboat rescue team

5 fire and rescue helicopter

6 police officer

Getting better

1 Doctors who are experts at treating sick children are called pediatricians.

2 Nurses care for sick people.

3 Doctors are trained to figure out why we feel unwell and make us feel better.

If we feel unwell, these specially trained people take care of us and help us to recover. There are lots of different jobs in medicine—here are a few of them. **Maybe one day you could help someone get better?**

5 The pharmacist's job is to give people the medicines that doctors say they need.

4 A midwife helps to deliver babies.

6 Surgeons perform operations to help sick people get better.

7 A radiologist scans the inside of your body to find out where the problem may be.

1 pediatrician

2 nurse

3 doctors

4 midwife

5 pharmacist

6 surgeon

7 radiologist

Working with animals

1 A veterinarian helps treat animals and gives advice on how to keep them healthy.

2 Veterinary assistants take care of animals after they've had operations.

3 Most dogs need to be walked at least once a day to stay fit and well—that's what dog walkers do!

4 Zookeepers look after the animals in a zoo—from ants to zebras!

It's not just people who need experts to keep them fit and well—animals need carers, too! All of these jobs help treat and protect our feathered, furry, and four-legged friends.

5 Pet shelter volunteer staff give up their time to look after animals who need a home.

6 Pet groomers clip claws and wash and trim fur to keep pets tidy and clean.

7 A beekeeper collects the honey that bees produce in a beehive. *Buzz!*

8 Wildlife sanctuary staff care for animals in protected habitats.

1 veterinarian

2 veterinary assistant

3 dog walker

4 zookeeper

5 pet shelter volunteers

6 pet groomer

7 beekeeper

8 wildlife sanctuary staff

Conserving our planet

1 Marine biologists study our seas and oceans.

2 Ecology educators explain how and why we should look after our planet.

3 Ocean cleanup crews clear trash from the water.

Conservationists are people who want to preserve and improve the different environments that people and wildlife live in. Some parts of their job involve making people aware of problems, and other parts are all about making the planet a better place for everyone. **What could you do to help?**

4 If you want someone to plan, manage, and reduce waste, you need a recycling officer!

5 Wildlife conservationists protect things in the natural world.

7 A botanist is an expert in plants.

6 Ornithologists are bird experts.

1 marine biologists

2 ecology educator

3 ocean cleanup crew

4 recycling officer

5 wildlife conservationists

6 ornithologist

7 botanist

Spread the word!

1

Reporters sometimes interview people live on TV!

2 Journalists investigate news stories and write about them for newspapers, online media, TV, and radio.

3

Influencers show and describe the things they like doing to people watching online.

How does everyone find out what is going on in the world? From sports events to the decisions that are made by different countries' leaders, there is someone to report on every subject under the sun. **What interesting news would you like to tell the world about?**

4 Bloggers and vloggers use words and videos to tell us about things they are interested in.

5 Newspaper editors decide what stories and information will go in the newspaper that day.

6 News broadcasters read the news so that we know what's going on!

7 A camera operator films news or events as they happen.

1 reporter		**4** blogger and vlogger		**7** camera operator	
2 journalist		**5** newspaper editor			
3 influencer		**6** news broadcaster			

Let's read!

1 An author comes up with ideas and writes all the words in the book.

2 Editors work with the author on the story and to make sure the text is correct.

3 An illustrator creates the pictures you're looking at now!

4 Designers create the cover and organize all the pages inside.

Have you ever wondered how many people are needed to create a book? Publishing is what happens when a book is produced, and it involves lots of people with special skills. **Maybe one day you'll have a job working on books?**

5 Production staff make sure the book is printed correctly.

6 Warehouse staff pack and send the books to bookstores.

7 Sales and marketing staff tell the world about new books.

8 A bookseller tells people about the book and sells it to them.

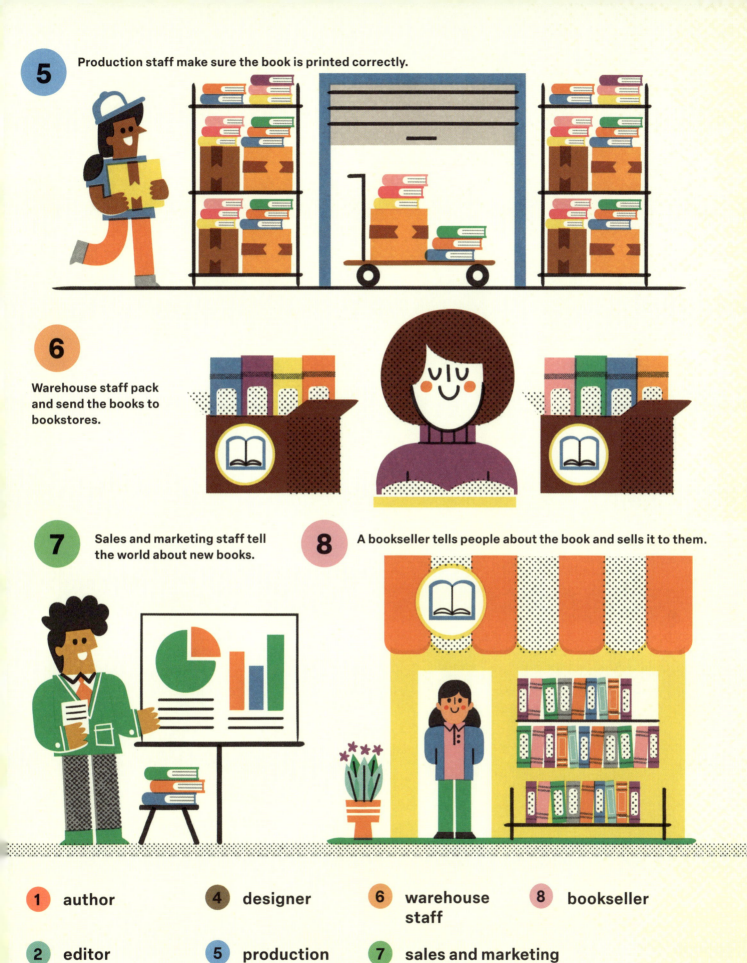

1 author

2 editor

3 illustrator

4 designer

5 production staff

6 warehouse staff

7 sales and marketing staff

8 bookseller

Look at this!

1 Mural makers work BIG!

2 Painters may paint landscapes or portraits—anything can be created in paint.

3 Textile designers create fabrics for fashion designers to work with.

4 Photographers use a camera to take fantastic photos of what they see.

Artists and designers create amazing works of art that make our world more beautiful and interesting to look at. They use a whole array of different materials to turn something simple into something amazing. **Which kind of artist would you like to be?**

5

Graphic designers use computer software to create images and symbols to convey a message.

6

Sculptors use stone, wood, or even ice to create statues.

A product designer decides what objects should look like and how they work.

7 Potters make things from clay.

8

1	mural maker	**3**	textile designer	**5**	graphic designer	**7**	potter
2	painter	**4**	photographer	**6**	sculptor	**8**	product designer

Put on a show!

2 The lighting crew uses lights to create atmosphere and effects on the stage or screen.

1 The director on a movie set tells everyone what to do.

3 A scriptwriter writes the words for the actors to say on stage, in movies, and on TV.

4 Prop makers create all the things that help tell the story you see, from cups to jewelry!

SUNSET

Everything you watch on TV or at the movies, or see performed onstage or in the street takes a lot of different skills to create. **Which of these entertainment jobs would you be good at?**

5 Set decorators design and make a show's scenery.

6 Makeup artists have the skills to transform how people look!

8 An actor plays a character and pretends to be them onstage or on-screen.

7 Costume designers design and make the actors' clothes for the stage or screen.

1 director

4 prop maker

7 costume designer

2 lighting crew

5 set decorator

8 actor

3 scriptwriter

6 makeup artist

Music makers

2 A conductor keeps all the musicians in an orchestra in time so the music sounds perfect!

1 Composers write music and songs for musicians to play and sing.

3 Sound engineers help record the music in a studio and make sure it sounds good.

ON AIR

4 The person who introduces the songs played on the radio is the disc jockey, or DJ.

Our world would be a very dull—and quiet!—place without music, but there are many jobs you can do even if you can't sing or play an instrument! **Let's make some noise!**

6 A band leader is the head of a group of musicians that play pop, jazz, blues, brass, or big band sounds.

5 Musicians play instruments—from small violins to very large drums!

7 DJs play music for people at parties or events.

8 Talent scouts find new musicians.

1 composer

2 conductor

3 sound engineer

4 disc jockey

5 musician

6 band leader

7 DJ

8 talent scout

IT experts!

1 Software designers create the different apps and programs we use.

2 UX (User Experience) designers make using apps and websites easier!

3 IT (Information Technology) support staff help people fix tech problems.

One of the ways we work and play today is on a computer. All the things you see on your computer screen—and the screen itself—have been designed by someone. And another person needs to know how to fix things when they go wrong!

4 Animators make movies using digital technology.

5 SFX (Special Effects) teams use digital technology to make imaginary things look real!

6 Game developers create computer games.

1 software designer

2 UX designer

3 IT support staff

4 animator

5 SFX team

6 game developer

We design spaces

1 Architects design buildings and think about how they are to be used—homes, stores, schools, and train stations.

2 Civil engineers figure out how to build things safely.

Look around you. The place you are in right now was designed by someone who had an idea about how it should look and what it would be used for. Everything from its shape and size to the materials that were used was carefully thought about by these clever people.

3 Landscape architects make outdoor spaces useful and welcoming.

4 Interior designers decide how the inside of buildings should look.

1 architect

2 civil engineer

3 landscape architect

4 interior designer

We build places

1 Construction workers dig out the foundations and build the walls of buildings.

2 Scaffolders put up scaffolding platforms around buildings so workers can access higher outside levels safely.

3 Roofers put roofs on new buildings and fix damage to old ones.

Builders take the plans drawn by architects and turn their drawings into spaces to live, play, learn, and work in. There is a whole team of people involved in every stage of each building project. **Have you ever seen inside a construction site?**

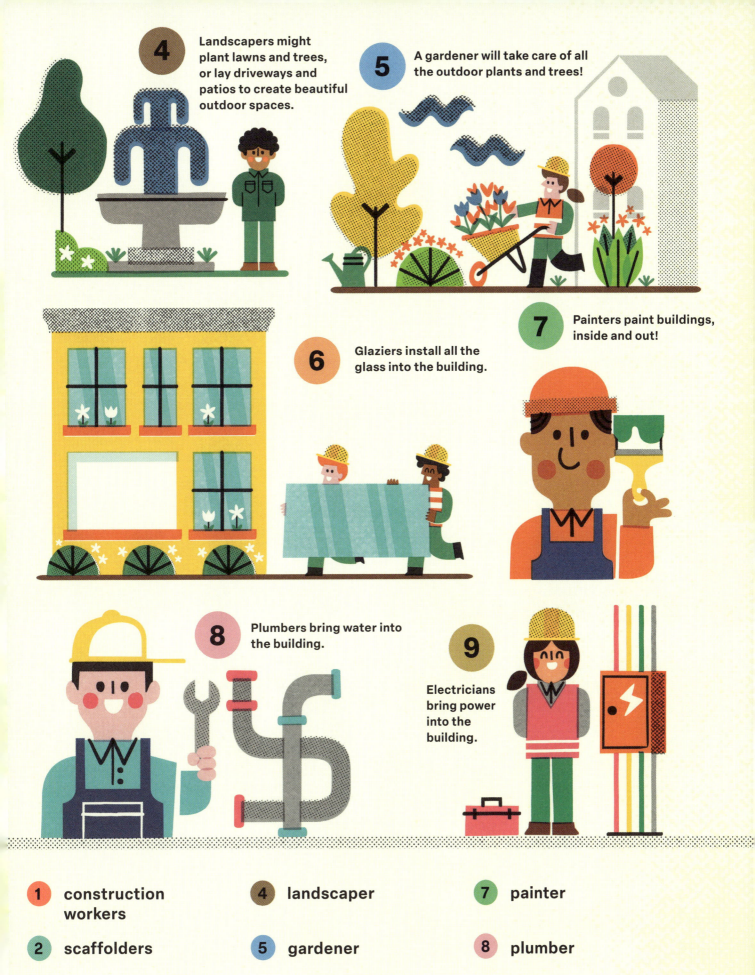

4 Landscapers might plant lawns and trees, or lay driveways and patios to create beautiful outdoor spaces.

5 A gardener will take care of all the outdoor plants and trees!

6 Glaziers install all the glass into the building.

7 Painters paint buildings, inside and out!

8 Plumbers bring water into the building.

9 Electricians bring power into the building.

1 construction workers

2 scaffolders

3 roofers

4 landscaper

5 gardener

6 glaziers

7 painter

8 plumber

9 electrician

A world of wellness

1 People go to beauticians to improve the way they look.

2 *Snip! Snip!* Hairdressers cut, color, and style hair.

3 Nutritionists know all about healthy eating.

4 A fitness coach helps people stay fit and healthy through exercise.

These are some of the many people who keep our minds and bodies looking and feeling good. They play an important part in making a busy world feel less stressful.

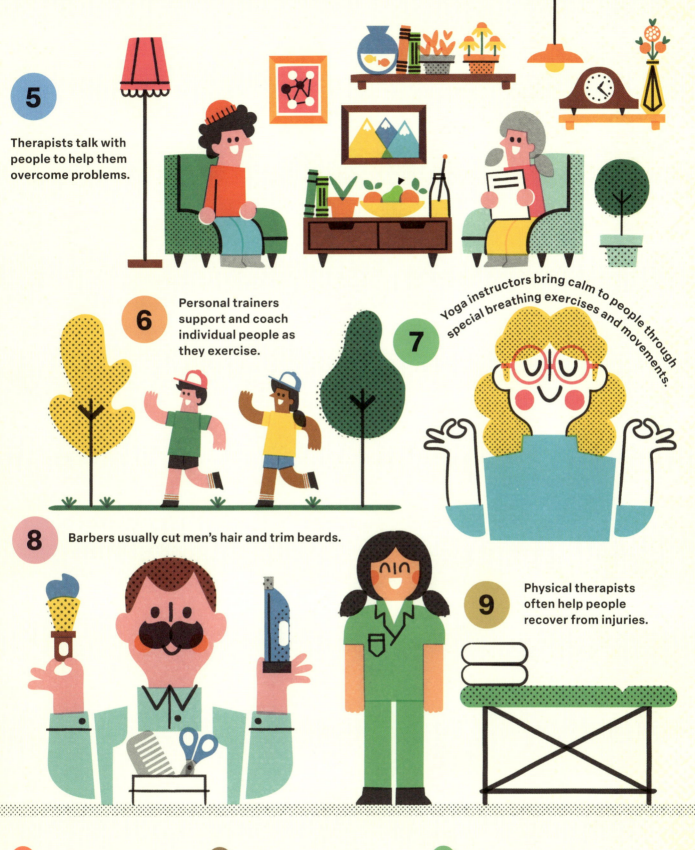

5

Therapists talk with people to help them overcome problems.

6 Personal trainers support and coach individual people as they exercise.

7 Yoga instructors bring calm to people through special breathing exercises and movements.

8 Barbers usually cut men's hair and trim beards.

9 Physical therapists often help people recover from injuries.

1	beautician	**4**	fitness coach	**7**	yoga instructor
2	hairdresser	**5**	therapist	**8**	barber
3	nutritionist	**6**	personal trainer	**9**	physical therapist

Time to eat!

1 Sushi chefs use fresh vegetables, rice, and raw fish to make delicious Japanese food.

2 Diner chefs prepare quick-to-cook food.

3 Food truck vendors drive up to places and cook and serve food from their trucks.

Whether it's spicy food, a plate of pancakes, or a burger, there is a chef for every type of meal or drink you can imagine. **What do you like to eat and drink?**

4 A baker makes bread, cakes, pastries, and desserts.

5 Baristas serve up hot and cold coffee.

6 Ice cream scoopers make delicious desserts from ice cream, frozen yogurt, or sorbet.

7 Juice bar staff make healthy juices and smoothies to order.

1 sushi chef

2 diner chef

3 food truck vendor

4 baker

5 barista

6 ice cream scooper

7 juice bar staff

Farm to fork

1 Farmers grow grain, fruit, or vegetable crops, or raise animals like cows or pigs.

2 Fishermen usually go out in boats to catch fish.

3 Much of the food we eat is collected from orchards and fields by fruit and vegetable pickers.

Farmers and fishermen have a vital role to play in making sure everyone gets enough to eat. Their produce needs to be grown, picked, packed, and sent to stores for us to buy. **Let's find out who else is involved!**

4 Delivery drivers take the food from farms to places where it can be bought and sold.

5 Farm stand staff sell goods from a farm directly to customers.

6 Farmers market workers make beautiful displays of fresh produce.

7 Factory workers turn these ingredients into the food we see in supermarkets.

1 farmer

2 fisherman

3 fruit and vegetable pickers

4 delivery driver

5 farm stand staff

6 farmers market worker

7 factory worker

At your service

1 Grocers sell fresh fruit, vegetables, and other food products.

3 A gas station attendant puts fuel in people's cars.

2 Who chooses what goes on display at a museum or gallery? That's the job of a museum curator.

4 Florists sell and deliver flowers.

Let's take a stroll through your town and see who's hard at work.
These people help make where you live a cool place to spend time.

5 If you need to find a book at your local library, a librarian will help you.

6 Sanitation workers and street cleaners make sure where we live stays clean.

7 Movie theater ushers help people buy tickets and find their seats.

8 Delivery drivers bring food like pizza to our doorstep!

9 Busy salespeople help us find things to buy in all kinds of stores.

1 grocer

2 museum curator

3 gas station attendant

4 florist

5 librarian

6 sanitation worker and street cleaner

7 movie theater usher

8 delivery driver

9 salesperson

Traveling around

1 Delivery drivers drop off everything from socks to food on your doorstep.

2 Postal workers deliver mail and packages.

3 Let's hop in a cab! The taxi driver will take us where we need to go.

4 Long-distance truck drivers often move items from one state to another.

Knock! Knock! There's somebody at the door! But have you ever stopped to think about all the different jobs that involve traveling from place to place?

5 Up, up, and away! Pilots fly and land aircraft.

6 Train engineers take us on short and long railway trips.

7 Bicycle messengers are a way to get important items somewhere fast.

8 Movers will take your belongings to your new home if you move.

1	delivery driver	**4**	truck driver	**7**	bicycle messenger
2	postal worker	**5**	pilot	**8**	mover
3	taxi driver	**6**	train engineer		

Working off-planet!

1 Astronauts are trained to travel in a spacecraft. Five, four, three, two, one . . . Liftoff!

2 Engineers on the International Space Station work 250 miles (402km) above our heads.

3 Astronomers study the universe to help us understand our solar system and other galaxies.

Some jobs are simply out of this world! Here are some roles that could take you off the Earth's surface and into a galaxy far, far away . . . or help you become an awesome space scientist.

4 Meteorologists study the Earth's atmosphere and oceans to predict weather patterns.

5 Astrochemists figure out what stars and comets are made from.

1 astronaut   **3** astronomer   **5** astrochemist

2 engineer   **4** meteorologist

Here to help

1 A preschool assistant takes care of small children before they start school.

2 A tai chi instructor trains people in this Chinese martial art.

3 A music therapist uses music and sound to improve people's well-being.

Whether you're young or old, there's someone out there whose job it is to make your life safer and more interesting. **From spending time together to trying out a new hobby, who would you like to learn from?**

4 Dance teachers teach people to dance.

5 Sports coaches help people achieve their best at a sport.

6 Elder care workers look after or give support to older people.

7 Want to learn to paint, draw, or create something cool? An arts and crafts teacher can make that happen.

1 preschool assistant

2 tai chi instructor

3 music therapist

4 dance teacher

5 sports coach

6 elder care worker

7 arts and crafts teacher

43

Back to school

1 The principal is the head of a school.

2 Counselors talk with anyone who wants to discuss their problems, thoughts, or feelings.

3 Teachers share their knowledge so that students can develop new skills and learn about different subjects.

$$3 \times 1 = 3$$
$$3 \times 2 = 6$$
$$3 \times 3 = 9$$

One of the most important jobs is that of a teacher—after all, without them, we might not even know how to read this book! Many other people work in schools, too. **Let's keep learning together, whatever job you choose!**

4 Office staff order supplies and equipment.

5 Kitchen staff prepare school meals.

6 Classroom assistants suppport teachers and look after students.

7 Janitors keep schools clean and tidy.

1 principal		**4** office staff		**7** janitor	
2 counselor		**5** kitchen staff			
3 teacher		**6** classroom assistant			